The
Presidents
of the
United States

The Marshall Cavendish illustrated history of
The Presidents
of the
United States

Written by
Ruth Oakley

Illustrated by
Steve Lucas and Tim Woodcock-Jones

MARSHALL CAVENDISH
New York · London · Toronto · Sydney

Library Edition Published 1990

© Marshall Cavendish Limited 1990
© DPM Services Limited 1990

Published by Marshall Cavendish Corporation
147, West Merrick Road
Freeport
Long Island
N.Y. 11520

Series created by Graham Beehag Book Design
Designed by Graham Beehag
Produced by DPM Services Limited

Library of Congress Cataloging-in-Publication Data

Oakley, Ruth.
  The Marshall Cavendish illustrated history of presidents of the United States / by Ruth Oakley
    p. cm.
  Includes indexes.
  Summary: Places each American preesident in a historical context and discusses his life, with an emphasis on his political activity and presidential term.
  ISBN 1-85435-144-3 (set)
  1. Presidents – United States – Biography – Juvenile literature. 2. United States – Politics and government – Juvenile literature.
[1. Presidents.] I. Title.
E176.8.025 1990
973'.0992 – dc20   89-17283
[B]   CIP
[920]   AC

Printed and bound in the United States of America by Lake Book Manufacturing Inc.

CONTENTS

Introduction

The outstanding men who served the United States as president in the beginning of her history as a nation achieved lasting greatness.

Afterward, there came a time of political in-fighting and compromise. Many of the men chosen for this highest office were able and dedicated. However, during the period between the beginning of the 1800s and the end of the Civil War, only one has achieved lasting fame. The name of Abraham Lincoln is forever linked with the ending of slavery in the United States, although in fact it was not achieved in his lifetime. It was not even what he considered his most important challenge.

Lincoln came to office when the southern states had already broken away from the Union to form the Confederacy. For all but five days of his time in office, his task was to fight and win the Civil War. He wrote, "The central issue pervading this struggle is the necessity of proving that popular government is not an absurdity. We must settle this question now, whether, in a free government, the minority have the right to break up the government whenever they choose."

The United States had struggled for more than half a century to earn the right to be recognized as an independent nation and to take its place as a world power. Throughout the years from 1845 to 1864, it threatened to tear itself apart.

There was a dangerous division of opinion, customs and economic necessity between the northern and southern states. The people of the industrial, manufacturing north with plentiful, immigrant labor saw no need for slaves. Many thought slavery was wrong in principle. Writers such as Ralph Waldo Emerson and Harriet Beecher Stowe led protests.

Southerners, however, depended on slaves to work the cotton plantations which were their livelihood. Slaves also gave them political power, because a slave counted as three-fifths of a vote for representation in Congress.

There had, in fact, been many southern leaders, particularly in Virginia, who disapproved of slavery in principle and who freed their own slaves. But they understood the social, economic and political problems which the sudden, compulsory abolition of slavery would bring to the whole southern farming way of life. They heard of bad living and working conditions in the factories of the northern industrialists, which made them all the more determined to preserve their own traditions and

The Battle of Vicksburg, 1863.

society. Transportation was still difficult, and the people of the north and south often had little real knowledge or understanding of each other's way of life.

Black laborers in Virginia.

Cotton is a crop which quickly exhausts the land on which it is grown. As land in the Deep South became worn out, there was a continual expansion of cotton plantations, and with them slavery, toward the west as territory was annexed from Mexico. Then, gold was discovered in California, creating a new drive further west.

As each new territory became populated and asked to be admitted to the Union as a state, the slavery issue came to the fore. If the state was to be free, the Southerners began to feel outnumbered in government. If it was to be slave, the anti-slave faction objected on principle. From Polk and Texas to Buchanan and Kansas, the dispute rumbled on. A series of compromises tried to reconcile the two viewpoints. It fell to Lincoln to deal with civil war when it finally came.

8

JAMES K. POLK

(1795-1849)

Eleventh President: 1845-1849

"The Continentalist"

Early years

James Knox Polk was born in 1795 near Charlotte, North Carolina, in Mecklenburg County. His father, Samuel, was a farmer, planter and surveyor of Irish descent. The ancestors of Jane Knox, his mother, had emigrated from Scotland. James was the eldest of their ten children. When he was eleven, the family moved to Tennessee. He graduated from the University of North Carolina with the highest honors in mathematics and classics. He decided to become a lawyer and was admitted to the Tennessee Bar when he was twenty-two. He became a successful advocate and was elected to the Tennessee legislature three years later. At the age of twenty-seven, he became a member of the U.S. House of Representatives.

Sarah Childress Polk

Sarah Childress and James Polk were married on New

During Polk's presidency, a million square miles of territory were added to the twenty-seven states which formed the Union when he took office.

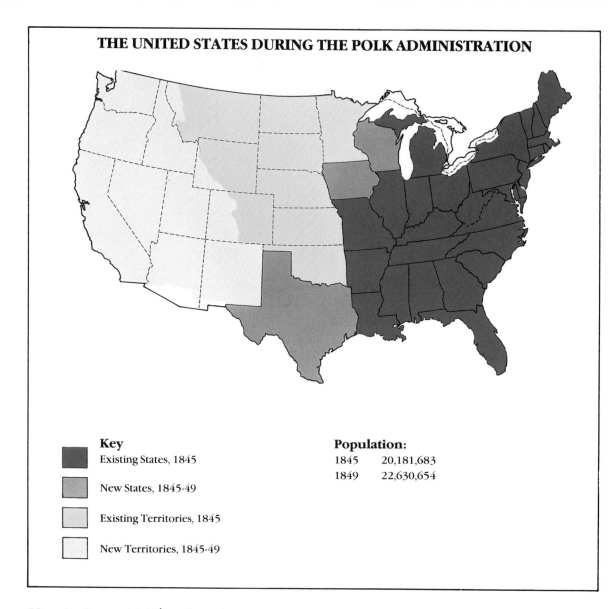

THE UNITED STATES DURING THE POLK ADMINISTRATION

Key
Existing States, 1845

New States, 1845-49

Existing Territories, 1845

New Territories, 1845-49

Population:
1845   20,181,683
1849   22,630,654

Year's Day, 1824, when he was twenty-eight and she was twenty. Sarah was the exceptionally well-educated daughter of wealthy Tennessee plantation owner, Captain Joel Childress, and a niece of President Andrew Jackson. The couple had no children.

Sarah was an intelligent and accomplished woman who took an active, although discreet, part in her husband's political success. She was a devout Presbyterian, and as hostess at the White House, her entertainments were sedate and sober. Nevertheless, she was popular and well-respected. She outlived her

> He translated into action the phrase, "Manifest Destiny," which was originally conceived by a reporter, John O'Sullivan. This meant that it was inevitable and desirable that the U.S. should spread across the whole continent of North America.

husband by forty-two years and was revered until her death in 1891.

"Young Hickory," the dark horse

Polk was a political protégé of his wife's uncle, Andrew Jackson, "Old Hickory," whose influence helped him gain the office of Speaker of the House of Representatives from 1835-9. Polk relinquished this position when he was elected Governor of Tennessee. He ran for re-election in 1841 and again in 1843, but was defeated on both occasions by the Whigs, the popular party at the time.

He declined Tyler's offer of a seat in his Cabinet, which left him free to run as the Democratic candidate for the presidency against the far better known Whig candidate, Henry Clay. Both Clay and Van Buren, the obvious Democratic candidate, opposed the annexation of Texas, which would almost certainly mean war with Mexico. It would also aggravate the problem of keeping a balance between "slave" and "non-slave" states in the Union. There was a three-way split, and Polk was elected by a narrow majority.

Polk's Presidency

Polk became the youngest President at the age of forty-nine. He announced that he had four main aims: a reduction of the tariff; the re-establishment of an independent treasury; the settlement of the Oregon boundary; and the gaining of California. He was opposed to internal improvements.

In 1846, the Walker Tariff Act began to reduce the

On the Oregon Trail.

After gold was discovered on the land of Sutter, a Swiss immigrant in California, 70,000 Americans set off to cross the continent and scour the streams and canyons in 1849. They were called the "Forty-niners."

tariff. The Independent Treasury Act of the same year enabled the U.S. government to take care of its own funds without the assistance of any banks.

In 1846, negotiations with England resulted in an agreement that the boundary of Oregon be fixed at the forty-ninth parallel except for a dip at Puget Sound, which gave Vancouver Island to the British. The U.S. got most of the Columbia River and the future states of Oregon, Washington and Idaho.

California was a province of Mexico, but in June, 1846, forty men set up the "Republic of California." A series of demonstrations followed. Then, in 1848, gold was discovered and the Gold Rush began.

John Tyler's last act as President had been to

If a prospector found gold in California he was then faced with the problem of transporting it back East.

Life in the gold mines of California was hard and primitive.

persuade Congress to accept the annexation of Texas in December, 1844. Mexico had refused to sell the territory, and Americans living there had rebelled and set up an independent republic under the governorship of Sam Houston.

Mexico threatened to declare war if Texas was annexed. Polk sent John Slidell to Mexico City to negotiate, but the Mexicans refused to receive him. Polk's reaction was to send an armed force to the southwestern border of Texas under the command of General Zachary Taylor. Polk ordered Taylor to push forward to the Rio Grande. The Mexicans regarded this act as an invasion of their territory.

In an attack in April, 1846, Mexican forces defeated a detachment of American cavalry. On May 11, 1848, Polk declared that the United States was at war with Mexico. Efforts to negotiate failed. Taylor achieved a decisive victory at Monterrey in September, 1846, and

Gold could also be
found by panning
the rivers and
streams.

defeated Santa Anna, the Mexican leader, at Buena Vista. General Winfield Scott marched from Vera Cruz to Mexico City with only about ten thousand troops and captured the capital.

The war was ended by the Treaty of Guadelupe Hidalgo on February 2, 1848. By its terms the Rio Grande became the boundary between the U.S. and Mexico. New Mexico, Upper California and parts of Utah, Nevada, Colorado and Arizona passed to the U.S. in return for fifteen million dollars.

Polk worked extremely hard as President. He achieved his main aims and then refused nomination for a second term. He retired to his home in Nashville,

where he died of cholera only three months after leaving office.

BIOGRAPHY BOX

James Knox Polk

Birthplace	Mecklenburg County, North Carolina
Date of birth	November 2, 1795
Education	University of North Carolina
Profession	Lawyer
Presidential term	March 4, 1845 to March 4, 1849
Party	Democratic
Place of death	Nashville, Tennessee
Date of death	June 15, 1849
Place of burial	Nashville, Tennessee

An attack on the gate at San Cosme during the Battle of Mexico in 1847.

ZACHARY TAYLOR
(1784-1850)

Twelfth President: 1849-1850

"Old Rough and Ready"

Family and upbringing

Zachary Taylor was born in Orange County, Virginia, on November 24, 1784. Both his parents were of English descent and were connected with prominent Virginia families. Zachary was the third of five sons and had three sisters as well.

When Zachary was a baby, his father, Colonel Richard Taylor, moved the family to Kentucky, where George Washington later appointed him as Collector of the port of Louisville. Kentucky was a wild and dangerous region. Zachary had little formal education, but learned self-reliance and was physically very fit. His brother was a lieutenant in the U.S. Army, and when he died, President Jefferson appointed Zachary in his place.

Taylor married Margaret Smith in 1810. She was the orphaned daughter of a Maryland planter and willingly shared Zachary's army postings. They had six children, of whom two girls died in childhood. This weakened Margaret's health, and by the time Zachary became President, she was a semi-invalid. Their married daughter, Betty Taylor Bliss, took on the formal social duties as the President's hostess.

Betty Taylor Bliss acted as hostess for her father during his residence at the White House.

Military career

Taylor never lost a battle. In the War of 1812, he fought off an attack on his garrison at Fort Harrison on the Wabash River in Indiana. His force of only fifty men were besieged by almost five hundred Indian warriors. He was also successful in the Black Hawk War of 1832.

In the Seminole War in Florida, Taylor defeated the Indians at the battle of Lake Ocheechobee and was made a Brigadier General. During this period, he also operated cotton plantations in Louisiana and Mississippi.

He was sent to Texas to protect it in case Mexico decided to "invade" it. War was declared by President Polk after a Mexican attack on a small force of American cavalry. Taylor won victories at Palo Alto and Resaca de la Palma. He occupied Monterrey after

American victory against Mexico at the Battle of Buena Vista in 1847.

Southern cotton plantations depended on slave labor. Here they feed a cotton press which screws the fiber down into bales ready to be carted to river boats for the journey to New Orleans.

fierce fighting and conquered the northeastern states of Mexico.

The final triumph of his military career — and the beginning of his political one — was his victory over the Mexican leader, General Santa Anna, at Buena Vista. Taylor had been ordered by President Polk to detach most of his regular troops to General Winfield Scott for an attack on Mexico City. The fighting at Buena Vista was fierce, and the battle hung in the

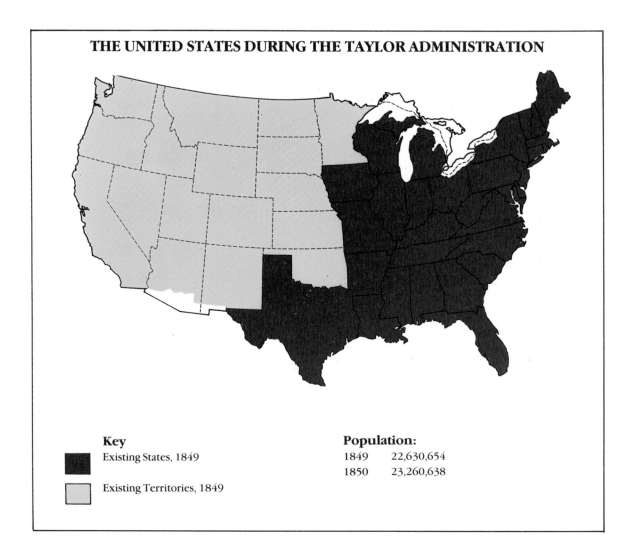

THE UNITED STATES DURING THE TAYLOR ADMINISTRATION

Key
Existing States, 1849

Existing Territories, 1849

Population:
1849   22,630,654
1850   23,260,638

balance for two days. Then the much larger Mexican force retired defeated. The Mexican losses were much greater than the 673 Americans who were killed and wounded.

Presidential candidate

Taylor had shown little interest in politics; he had no political experience and knew little about government or law. He said that he was a Whig, but he had never voted in any election. Still, he seemed to be an ideal candidate. He was personally popular as a military hero, and he had never made any statements of political policy to antagonize public opinion.

He was chosen by the Whig party as Presidential candidate in preference to Henry Clay, a much more able and experienced statesman, and Winfield Scott, his fellow general and Mexican War hero. The Democratic candidate was General Lewis Cass. Van Buren also stood as a "Free Soil" candidate. Taylor's success was due partly to this split in the opposition.

Taylor's Presidency and death

The problem which dominated Taylor's presidency was slavery, particularly with respect to new states admitted to the Union because of the victory over Mexico. In 1848, gold had been discovered in California, and the resulting Gold Rush quickly increased the population there. A separate state was formed, with a constitution which prohibited slavery.

This horrified the southern states, who depended on slaves for their political power and their wealth. They feared that if the non-slave states gained power in Congress, they would abolish the right to have slaves at all. Many Southerners threatened that, unless California was split into two states, of which one was and one was not a slave state, they would secede from the Union. Taylor was opposed to secession and warned that he would go to war against any rebellion.

Clay, as so often in the past, put forward a series of compromise measures, but Taylor did not agree with them. His solution was to admit California and New Mexico and allow them to decide the issue of slavery for themselves. He died while the measures were still being discussed.

As a general and professional soldier, Taylor showed great calmness and presence of mind in battle. He liked to find a high point where he could sit on his charger, Whitey, to watch the progress of the battle. Once, when his officers tried to persuade him to withdraw because he was exposing himself unnecessarily to the danger of being shot, he replied, "Let us ride up nearer and then their balls will go over us."

BIOGRAPHY BOX

Zachary Taylor

Birthplace	Orange County, Virginia
Date of birth	November 24, 1784
Education	Self-educated
Profession	Soldier
Presidential term	March 5, 1849 to July 9, 1850
Party	Whig
Place of death	Washington, D.C.
Date of death	July 9, 1850
Place of burial	Louisville, Kentucky

Cotton bales in New Orleans ready to be loaded aboard the ships which would transport them to Europe were a familiar sight during the mid-nineteenth century.

He attended Independence Day ceremonies on an extremely hot July 4, 1850, at the Washington Monument, which was being built. When he went home, he drank cold milk and ate cherries. A few days later, he died of acute gastroenteritis.

MILLARD FILLMORE

(1800-1874)

Thirteenth President: 1850-1853

A self-made man of humble origins

The Vice-President who took office after Zachary Taylor's unexpected death in 1850 was very little known. The prominent statesmen of the time were still Henry Clay and Daniel Webster, although they were both now old men. Millard Fillmore was a New Yorker of humble origins. He was born, the second of nine children, in a log cabin on the frontier in Locke, New York, on January 7, 1800. His father, Nathaniel, was a farmer of English descent.

Young Millard had little schooling, as his help was needed around the farm. He was apprenticed at the age of fifteen to a clothier and fuller to learn the trade of dressing cloth and dyeing and carding wool. Fillmore, however, was ambitious. By teaching, he managed to buy his freedom and to pay his own way to study law. He was admitted to the Bar of New York in 1823 and became very successful.

Family life

In 1826, he married Abigail Powers, a schoolteacher from Saratoga County, New York. They had met when Millard was her student at an academy in New Hope in

In his childhood, Fillmore had little opportunity to read. In the log cabin where he was born, there were only a Bible and a hymnbook. He said he did not see a copy of Shakespeare, "Robinson Crusoe" or a map of the United States until he was nineteen. He loved books and built up his own library of about five thousand volumes. He persuaded Congress to provide money for books for the White House library, which Abigail chose and organized.

1819, but could not afford to marry until Millard had made his way as a lawyer. They had a son and a daughter, Mary Abigail. "Abby" took over many of the formal entertaining duties at the White House when Fillmore became President. Mrs. Fillmore's health was delicate, and she preferred reading and music to society.

Despite her poor health, Abigail attended the outdoor events surrounding President Pierce's inauguration ceremonies in 1853 in very cold weather. She caught a chill which developed into pneumonia, and she died a month later. Millard was to bear another blow when "Abby" also died, aged only twenty-two, within a year of her mother's death. Fillmore married again in 1858. His bride was Mrs. Caroline C. McIntosh, a wealthy and childless widow, who outlived him.

Political background

Fillmore was elected to the N.Y. State Assembly from 1829-32 and represented New York in the House of Representatives from 1833-35 and from 1837-43. As Chairman of the Ways and Means Committee, he favored a protective tariff and internal improvements. He supported John Quincy Adams in measures against the increase of slavery. He failed to become Governor of New York, but was made State Comptroller.

This northern background made him a good Vice-

Presidential candidate for the Whig party to balance
to the southern cotton plantation owner and soldier,
Zachary Taylor. Also, he was easy-going and well-liked

**Every Southern
town had its slave
dealer.**

SLAVES FOR SALE
WITHOUT RESERVE

BY PRICE, BIRCH & Co

WILL BE AUCTIONED

FRIDAY Aug 14th

TERMS CASH.
ALSO

Harriet Beecher Stowe brought the evils of slavery to everyone's attention in her best-seller, "Uncle Tom's Cabin," which told the story of the slave girl, Topsy.

and had not made political enemies or antagonized the voters.

His Presidency

When Fillmore took over the presidency, Congress was still trying to solve the problems of admitting California and New Mexico to the Union, especially the question of whether or not they should be allowed to own slaves. Clay's Omnibus Bill, supported by Webster, was an effort to reach a compromise. Taylor had opposed its various measures, but Fillmore supported and signed them. He disliked slavery, but felt it his duty to be president of the whole country. He wanted to bridge the gap between north and south

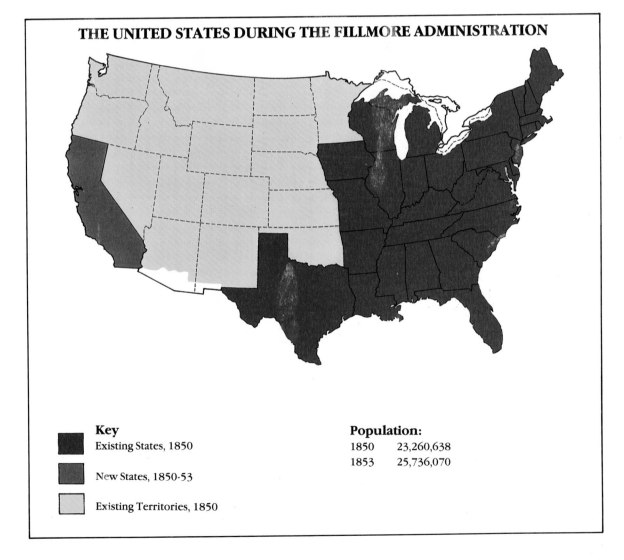

THE UNITED STATES DURING THE FILLMORE ADMINISTRATION

Key
Existing States, 1850

New States, 1850-53

Existing Territories, 1850

Population:
1850   23,260,638
1853   25,736,070

and to prevent the bloodshed which armed conflict was sure to bring.

Although the Acts saved the Union for the time being, one of them, a severe law against fugitive slaves passed in 1850, was very unpopular. It spelled the end of Fillmore's political career. The Whig party lost support, and the Democrats became stronger. General Winfield Scott, the Whig presidential candidate in 1852, was soundly defeated, and the party passed into obscurity.

During Fillmore's presidency, Commodore Perry was sent to Japan to open up the country to American trade.

Later life

Fillmore retired to Buffalo, taking three trips to tour Europe. He refused to join the new Republican party. In 1856, he accepted the presidential nomination of the "American" party, but was overwhelmingly defeated and never sought public office again. He was critical of President Lincoln's conduct of the Civil War. Millard Fillmore died of a stroke in 1874.

BIOGRAPHY BOX

Millard Fillmore

Birthplace	Locke, New York
Date of birth	January 7, 1800
Education	Self-educated
Profession	Lawyer
Presidential term	July 10, 1850 to March 4, 1853
Party	Whig
Place of death	Buffalo, New York
Date of death	March 8, 1874
Place of burial	Buffalo, New York

FRANKLIN PIERCE
(1804-1869)

Fourteenth President: 1853-1857

A dark horse President

Franklin Pierce was another President who had previously been virtually unknown in the political life of the United States. The Democrats needed as their presidential candidate a man who had made no enemies, who could win support from north and south and who could gain a two-thirds majority of the nominating convention. Pierce became the unanimous choice of the forty-ninth ballot. The Whig party was in decline, and its candidate General Winfield Scott, was soundly defeated in the 1852 election.

Pierce was a good-looking and charming man, but he had never sought high office. He proved unable to solve the intractable problem of the divisions in the Union between north and south.

Early life and marriage

Born in 1804 at Hillsboro, New Hampshire, Pierce

The poet, Henry Wadsworth Longfellow, and the writer, Nathaniel Hawthorne, were at Bowdoin College at the same time as Pierce.

"Border Ruffians" from Missouri crossed into Kansas to vote for a pro-slavery legislature in the elections.

was the sixth child of eight born to General Benjamin Pierce, soldier in the American Revolution, farmer and twice Governor of New Hampshire, and his second wife Anne Kendrick Pierce.

After graduating from Bowdoin College, Franklin became a successful lawyer and entered politics. He was a member of the Lower House of the New Hampshire Legislature from 1829-33. As a member of the U.S. House of Representatives from 1833-7, he supported President Andrew Jackson.

In 1834, he married Jane Means Appleton against her family's wishes. She was shy, and her health was delicate. She discouraged Franklin's participation in politics and disliked the social life in Washington. Their first son died when he was just three days old, and when Jane gave birth to another boy, her feelings were an important factor in his decision to quit politics and return to New Hampshire. Sadly, this son too died the next year. Pierce resigned from the Senate in 1842, having entered as its youngest member. He also refused President Polk's offer of the post of Attorney General.

He fought bravely in the Mexican War, reaching the rank of Brigadier General. He took part in the advance on Mexico City. On his safe return, he lived for four years in quiet happiness with Jane and their third son, Benjamin, at Concord. When she heard the news of his Presidential nomination, Jane fainted. Shortly before Pierce's inauguration, the family was involved in a railroad accident. Benny was killed before his parents' eyes. Devastated, Jane found her social obligations as White House hostess more painful than she thought possible, but she found some comfort in religion and did her best to do her duty.

After Franklin's final retirement from politics, the couple went abroad to try to improve Jane's health, but with no success. She died in 1863.

His Presidency

When Pierce became President in 1853, the problems between the North and the South seemed to have been solved by the Compromise of 1850 which Pierce had supported. There was soon a new source of disagreement: Kansas. The Kansas-Nebraska Bill suggested the admission of the new states to the

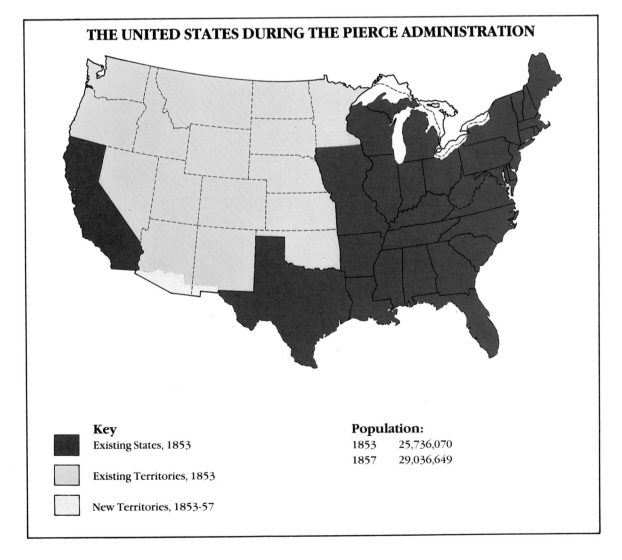

THE UNITED STATES DURING THE PIERCE ADMINISTRATION

Key

Existing States, 1853

Existing Territories, 1853

New Territories, 1853-57

Population:
1853   25,736,070
1857   29,036,649

Union with the freedom to decide for themselves whether or not to allow slavery. This would break the conditions of the Missouri Compromise of 1820, which had laid down that there were to be no slave states north and west of the southern boundary of Missouri. So, the Compromise was declared to be void.

The question of slavery came sharply back into focus, and fierce disagreements were stirred up once more. The Republican party came into being, composed of different political groups who were all anti-slavery. Supporters of both factions poured into Kansas, and fighting broke out between them. Eventually, the state framed a pro-slavery constitution which Pierce was prepared to accept. In 1856, he sent federal troops and a new Governor to Kansas, but the problem was not solved during his administration.

Pierce did have some success in foreign policy. The Gadsden Purchase in 1853 bought parts of south Arizona and New Mexico from Mexico for ten million dollars to allow a railroad running across the continent to be built. There were rumors that America was trying to buy, or take by force, Hawaii, San Domingo, Alaska and Cuba. There were difficulties with Britain over her efforts to recruit Americans to fight in the Crimean War and over her interference in the affairs of Nicaragua.

Later life

Pierce was not nominated for a second term. In his

BIOGRAPHY BOX

Franklin Pierce

Birthplace	Hillsboro, New Hampshire
Date of birth	November 23, 1804
Education	Bowdoin
Profession	Lawyer
Presidential term	March 4, 1853 to March 4, 1857
Party	Democratic
Place of death	Concord, New Hampshire
Date of death	October 8, 1869
Place of burial	Concord, New Hampshire

Wilson Chinn, a branded slave from Louisiana, displays some of the instruments used to punish slaves.

later years, he had problems with alcoholism and ill health. His criticism of President Lincoln during the Civil War earned him the title of "Copperhead," a contemptuous name for Northerners who supported the south, so called because the copperhead snake strikes without warning. He died in 1869.

JAMES BUCHANAN

(1791-1868)

Fifteenth President: 1857-1861

Family background and early life

James Buchanan, the second of eleven children, was born in a log cabin near Cove Gap, Pennsylvania, in 1791. His father, an Irish immigrant, was a farmer and merchant. After his schooling at Mercersburg, James went to Dickinson College, Carlisle. He excelled at athletics as well as doing well academically. He began his law practice in 1812, but left to enlist in the army after the capture of Washington, D.C., by the British in the War of 1812.

He was a successful lawyer and had considerable political experience. He served in the Pennsylvania House of Representatives, the U.S. House of Representatives and the U.S. Senate, to which he was twice re-elected. President Andrew Jackson sent him as minister to Russia, and he was minister to Great Britain during President Pierce's administration. In President Polk's cabinet he was Secretary of State. He was elected President in a three-way fight with Fremont and Fillmore.

His fiancée, Anne C. Coleman, had died in 1819 after the couple had quarreled. It was rumored, but never confirmed, that she had committed suicide. Her father returned, unopened, a letter which Buchanan wrote asking to be allowed to see her body and attend

A slave family outside their log cabin.

her funeral. James Buchanan was the only bachelor president. When he became president, his niece, Miss Harriet Lane, acted as a charming and graceful hostess in his White House.

Buchanan gave his opinion on slavery as, "I believe it to be a great political and a great moral evil. I thank God my lot has been cast in a state where it does not exist. But while I entertain these opinions, I know it is an evil at present without a remedy."

PERSECUTED VIRTUE.

An illustration from "Uncle Tom's Cabin."

Slavery and Kansas

The major problem of Buchanan's presidency was the question of slavery, especially the effects which admitting Kansas would have on the balance of free and slave states in the Union. At this time, world opinion and the feelings of the majority of the population in the United States were against slavery. In the southern states, however, the cotton plantations depended on black slave labor, and slave votes which were cast by the slave owners, guaranteed political influence. Whatever Buchanan may have thought about the morality of slavery, his legal background made him content to accept the authority of law on the matter.

He was an acceptable presidential candidate for the Democratic party to a great extent because he had been abroad, as Minister for Great Britain, when the deep disagreement and argument as to whether or not Kansas should be admitted to the Union had taken place.

Kansas was allowed to retain its legal right to a constitution which permitted slavery and to join the

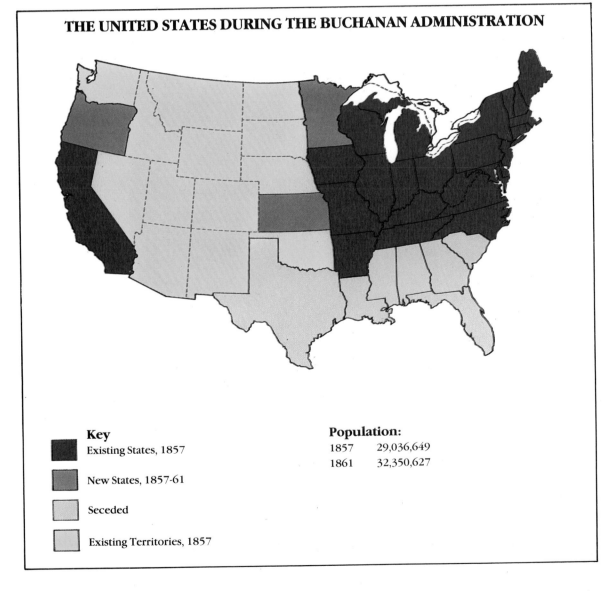

THE UNITED STATES DURING THE BUCHANAN ADMINISTRATION

Key

Existing States, 1857

New States, 1857-61

Seceded

Existing Territories, 1857

Population:

1857   29,036,649

1861   32,350,627

Life in the fields was hard.

Union. This decision caused anger and bitterness in the north. In 1861, Kansas was finally admitted to the Union as a free state, after Stephen Douglas opposed Buchanan and argued that the matter should be decided by a fair and free vote of the citizens of Kansas themselves.

The Dred Scott Decision was a legal verdict against the case of a black man who claimed that he had become free as the result of a stay in the territory which was declared to be free by the Missouri Compromise. This ruling meant that slave owners could take their slaves to territories to work for them. It confirmed that, under U.S. law, a slave was just like any other property of his master and had no legal rights. The Panic of 1857 temporarily took the attention of the northern industrialists away from the slavery issue. Economic recession hit America, trade slumped and Buchanan did nothing to resolve the differences between north and south.

The situation was made even more difficult in 1859 when John Brown tried to lead a slave revolt. With the help of a small band of men, of whom five were black slaves, he captured the federal arsenal at Harpers Ferry and murdered some of the town's citizens. The operation was soon cut short by Colonel Robert E. Lee and a company of marines, but the anti-slave faction had gained a martyr.

John Brown was captured, tried for treason, convicted and executed.

The Confederate States of America

Anti-slavery sentiment continued to strengthen until the election in 1860 of the Republican Abraham Lincoln. When the results were announced, seven southern states seceded from the Union. South Carolina acted first, on December 20, 1860, despite

John Brown achieved lasting fame in the hymn dedicated to his memory.

The just man shall be in eternal remembrance

Gave his Life for the Liberation of the Slave.

U.S. Marines storm the engine house at Harpers Ferry.

The invention of the telegraph opened up the country to improved communications.

Buchanan's state of the Union message a few weeks earlier in which he had said that states had no right to secede.

Buchanan did not have enough military power or support from Congress to force South Carolina to reverse its decision. Compromise measures were suggested, but failed, and war became inevitable. In February, 1861, Jefferson Davis became President of the Confederate States of America.

After his presidency, Buchanan retired from active politics, although he continued to support the Union during the Civil War. From his home at Wheatland, Pennsylvania, he wrote the history of his administration. He died in 1868.

BIOGRAPHY BOX

James Buchanan

Birthplace	Franklin County, Pennsylvania
Date of Birth	April 23, 1791
Education	Dickinson College
Profession	Lawyer
Presidential term	March 4, 1857 to March 4, 1861
Party	Democratic
Place of death	Lancaster, Pennsylvania
Date of death	June 1, 1868
Place of burial	Lancaster, Pennsylvania

ABRAHAM LINCOLN

(1809-1865)

Sixteenth President: 1861-1865

Abraham Lincoln

"Honest Abe"

"A poor nobody"

This was how Abraham Lincoln described himself
when he married Mary Todd in 1842. He was born in
a log cabin near Hodgenville, Kentucky, in 1809. His
father, Thomas Lincoln, was a farmer and carpenter.
Both he and Abraham's mother, Nancy Hanks, were
born in Virginia of English descent. When Abraham
was eight, his father moved the family to Indiana,
which Lincoln described as "a wild region with many
bears and other wild creatures still in the woods."

Nancy Hanks died two years later, and he had very
little formal education. He attended five schools, but
for a total time of less than a year. Nevertheless, he
was an avid reader, encouraged by his stepmother,
Mrs. Sarah Bush Johnston, although she could not
herself read.

He worked on the family farm until he was
nineteen, when he was employed to take a boatload of
produce down the Ohio and Mississippi to New
Orleans. When Thomas moved the Lincoln family to
Illinois in 1829, Abraham went with them; but almost
two years later, at the age of 22, he left home and
became a clerk in a store in New Salem, Illinois.

He served briefly in the Black Hawk War in 1832 as

a captain of a local volunteer force. After the war, he went into partnership in a store. The business failed, with debts which took Lincoln fifteen years to pay off. In New Salem, he became Postmaster and a local surveyor while he studied law. He was called to the bar in 1837 and built up a successful practice.

Mary Todd Lincoln

Mary Todd was a lively, well-educated, intelligent and attractive young woman whose parents were important members of society in their home state of Kentucky. Her courtship with Abraham Lincoln was stormy: their engagement was broken on New Year's Day, 1841, and they were apart for eighteen months until they were reconciled with the help of a mutual friend. After their marriage, the couple lived in

Lincoln was brought up in a humble log cabin.

Lincoln splitting logs for fence rails.

Lincoln's nickname "The Rail Splitter" came from the time in Illinois when he took on a contract to split three thousand fence rails.

Springfield, Illinois, in a much poorer and more humble style than that to which Mary was accustomed. Four boys were born to them, of whom only one outlived them.

When Lincoln became President, Mary was the subject of much criticism from both sides of the Civil War. Southerners regarded her as a traitor to her family and upbringing; her brothers fought for the Confederates. Northerners felt that she was not to be trusted and accused her of being a southern spy. She was accused of extravagance in her entertaining at the White House. When she curtailed her activities after the death of her son, Willie, she was said not to be fulfilling her social obligations.

She was sitting next to her husband when he was shot and never recovered from her shock and grief. After her son, Tad, died in 1871, Mary became mentally ill and was declared legally insane. She died in 1882.

Lincoln's political career

Lincoln ran for the state legislature of Illinois in 1832, announcing that he was in favor of a national bank, internal improvements and a high protective tariff. Although he failed to be elected on this occasion, he succeeded in 1834 and in the next three biennial elections.

From 1847 to 1849, he was a Whig member of the U.S. House of Representatives for Illinois. He was not active in politics again until he was drawn back by his opposition to the Kansas-Nebraska Bill of 1854, sponsored by Stephen A. Douglas. This act attempted to annul the Missouri Compromise, which had stated that there was to be no slavery north of latitude 36°30. Repeal of the Missouri Compromise would enable

Kansas to have a pro-slavery government.

Lincoln's attitude to slavery at this time was, "If slavery is not wrong, then nothing is wrong." Nevertheless, he was essentially practical in his approach to the problem, recognizing that a gradual reduction in the numbers of slaves was the safest solution. It was also inevitable if no new states were allowed to hold slaves.

In addition, he felt that the slave trade between Africa, Britain and America should be stopped, but that the Fugitive Slave Law, which enabled owners to bring back slaves who had escaped to free states,

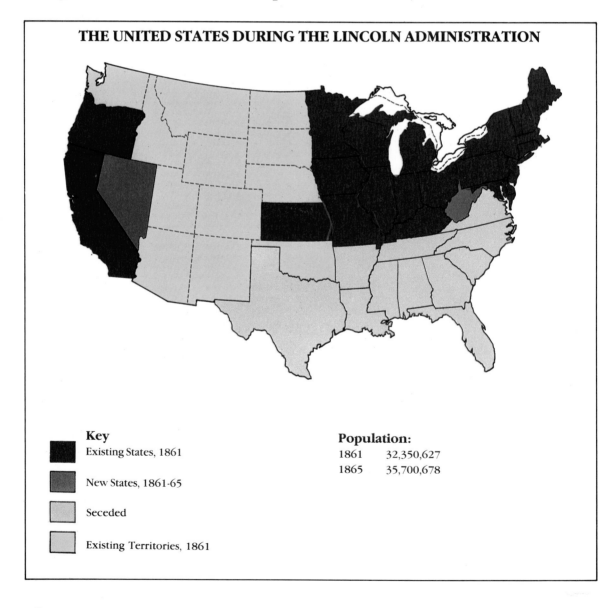

THE UNITED STATES DURING THE LINCOLN ADMINISTRATION

Key

Existing States, 1861

New States, 1861-65

Seceded

Existing Territories, 1861

Population:

| 1861 | 32,350,627 |
| 1865 | 35,700,678 |

should be maintained. Slavery should be allowed to remain in the states in which it already existed, but should not be allowed in new states wishing to join the Union. He did not support immediate emancipation, realizing the economic threat which would then face the south.

In 1856, he joined the newly formed Republican party, which was anti-slavery, but not abolitionist. He was nominated for the Senate in 1858, but lost to Stephen A. Douglas. Despite this setback, his performance in the campaign had been so impressive that he was adopted as the Republican party's presidential candidate in the 1860 election and won in November.

His victory alarmed the southern states, who regarded him as anti-slavery, and South Carolina seceded from the Union, quickly followed by Mississippi, Florida, Alabama, Georgia, Louisiana and Texas. These states formed the Confederate States of America under the Presidency of Jefferson Davis.

The Civil War

In his inaugural address, Lincoln warned, "The Union of these states is perpetual." He said that he had taken a solemn oath as President to "preserve, protect and defend" the government and that the decision whether or not there was to be civil war was in the hands of his countrymen, not his own.

When the Confederates fired on Fort Sumter in April, 1861, Civil War began. Lincoln took control of the Union's management of the war. He issued a proclamation that a state of insurrection existed and asked the states to provide 75,000 militia for ninety days to quell it. In May, he increased the U.S. Army, using two million dollars from government money to pay for war measures. He suspended Habeas Corpus.

Lincoln did not fight the war to end slavery: the important question, he felt passionately, was that the Union should be maintained. His determination and will to win was one of the main reasons for the North's eventual victory.

He avoided war with Britain in 1861 when he ordered the release of two Confederate envoys who had been arrested on a British ship which had been stopped on the high seas by a Union warship.

In September, 1862, Lincoln announced an Emancipation Proclamation, which ruled that from January 1, 1863, all slaves in rebel states would be

Battle of the Wilderness, 1864.

General Robert E. Lee was a brilliant commander for the Confederates.

free. It was a practical measure to help the Union by discouraging those slave states which had not yet joined the Confederacy from doing so. Nevertheless, it was a momentous decision, and one for which Lincoln is remembered.

According to the Constitution, the President is also Commander-in-Chief of the army and navy. Lincoln named and dismissed generals, although he did not generally interfere in their decisions of military strategy.

One of his main problems was to find capable and determined commanding officers. Lt. General Winfield Scott, a veteran of the War of 1812 and the Mexican War, was replaced by General George B.

McClellan. He in turn was replaced by General Ambrose E. Burnside and then Major General Hooker. Hooker was defeated at Chancellorsville in 1863 by troops led by Robert E. Lee. In July, 1863, his replacement, Major General George G. Meade, halted the Confederates under Robert E. Lee at Gettysburg and forced them to withdraw after a three-day battle.

At the same time, Major General Ulysses S. Grant, who had for weeks been besieging the strategically important town of Vicksburg on the Mississippi, finally succeeded in taking it. His victory cut the Confederate forces in half, and Grant was put in command of "the Armies of the United States."

Lincoln was re-elected in 1864, pledging reconstruction and reconciliation. On April 9, 1865, General Lee surrendered at the courthouse in Appomattox, Virginia, and the war was over.

After the war

Lincoln, as he had promised, tried to heal the wounds between north and south. He ordered the release of General Lee's two sons, who had been taken prisoner. On Good Friday, April 14, 1865, five days after Lee's surrender, President and Mrs. Lincoln were at Ford's Theater in Washington watching "Our American Cousin" as part of the victory celebrations. During the third act, John Wilkes Booth, an actor and

> **Lincoln's address, which he gave to dedicate the cemetery at Gettysburg, has become famous across the English-speaking world for its simple, but moving, dignity and its message of hope for the future.**
>
> **It concludes, "We here highly resolve that these dead shall not have died in vain, that this nation under God shall have a new birth of freedom, and that government of the people, by the people, for the people, shall not perish from the earth."**

Abraham Lincoln was shot by one of the actors while at the theater in Washington in April, 1865.

secessionist, entered the presidential box and shot Lincoln in the back of the head. The President was taken to a nearby house, where he died the next morning without regaining consciousness. He was the first American president to be assassinated. His body rested in state in the White House, viewed by thousands of mourners before being taken to Illinois for burial.

BIOGRAPHY BOX

Abraham Lincoln

Birthplace	Hardin County (now Larue County), Kentucky
Date of birth	February 12, 1809
Education	Self-educated
Profession	Lawyer
Presidential term	March 4, 1861 to April 15, 1865
Party	Republican
Place of death	Washington, D.C.
Date of death	April 15, 1865
Place of burial	Springfield, Illinois

GLOSSARY

admit to the Bar — allow to practice as a lawyer

Comptroller — the controller of financial affairs

constitution — laws and agreements which give a government its powers

emancipation — setting free, especially from slavery or unjust laws

faction — a group of people, especially in politics, who pursue their own self-interest

free state — a state whose constitution does not allow the holding of slaves

Habeas Corpus — a law which requires a person to be brought into court and charged to prevent him from being held in prison without being charged for an offense

insurrection — rebellion; resistance to an established authority

internal improvements — the building of roads, canals, railroads and other public works carried out by the federal government

legislature — the part of a country's government which makes its laws

militia — a military force, usually made up of ordinary citizens in an emergency to reinforce the regular army

protégé — a person who is guided and helped by another, usually older, person

province — a territory outside a country, but governed by it

recession — a decline in economic activity and prosperity

secede — withdraw from membership of a federation of states

surveyor — a person who measures land and draws maps and plans of it

tariff — a law imposing customs duties on exports and imports. In the U.S. in the nineteenth century, the tariff was used to protect home industry from foreign competition

territories — organized divisions of a country which does not have the full rights of a state